# The Field of Happiness

# The Field of Happiness

Poems by

Charles Rammelkamp

Cover design by Shay Culligan
Cover art by Gene McCormick

ISBN: 978-1-63980-126-8

Kelsay Books
502 South 1040 East, A-119
American Fork, Utah 84003
Kelsaybooks.com

# Acknowledgments

*433* "Poker Faces"

*The 5—2 Crime Poetry* "Boo Coo," "Denkmal," "Driving While Black," "Failure"

*Artifact Nouveau* "Study Buddies"

*Bindweed* "Breaking My Heart," "Now You're a Metaphor"

*Blood and Thunder* "Rashida and the Beast," "Sit-Down Comics"

*Brass City* "Grace"

*California Quarterly* "Denting My Self-Esteem"

*Chiron Review* "Father's Day on Facebook," "The Hairball," "Liking It Hot," "My First Sex Scandal," "A Pocketful of Mumbles," "River of No Return," "The Rusty Studebaker"

*Coe Review* "Fifi"

*Common Ground Review* "Rigoletto"

*Concho River Review* "Working Class Hero"

*Concrete Mist Press Anthology* "Age," "Destiny Foretold"

*Creosote* "You Made a Fool of Everyone"

*The Evening Street Review* "In the Clearing Stands a Boxer," "Justice," "Love" "Romance"

*Exit 13* "Celebrity," "Famous," "Paw Paw Charlie"

*Fictional Café* "The Crud," "The Plot Against America," "Trumplandia"

*Foliate Oak* "Maskenfreiheit"

*Gargoyle* "Joyeux Noël," "Swann's Way"

*The Great American Wise Ass Poetry Anthology* "A Close Shave"

*Homestead Review* "Backseat Blues," "Cutting My Losses," "Periodic Table"

*The Iconoclast* "Collision"

*The Indian River Review* "An Expert in the Field of Happiness"

*Main Street Rag* "Did That Just Happen?" "Mahlneid," "Stu"

*Meat for Tea* "A Whole New Gestalt"

*Medicinal Purposes* "Snow Day"

*Misfit Magazine* "Full Service," Meeting of the Titans"

*Nerve Cowboy* "Chode," "Cyber Immortality," "Low Cool," "What's a Solofie?"

*North of Oxford* "Alexander Pushkin Dies in a Duel," "Winter Tune-up"

*Off Course* "Disapproval," "Fighting Fair," "Full Disclosure," "Go, Cubs," "The Kindness of Strangers," "Registering to Vote"

*Outlaw Poetry* "Life Begins," "Pity"

*Pearl* "The Grifter," "Road Rage"

*Plainsongs* "Ribald"

*Presa* "The Metamorphosis"

*Quercus* "Heimlich"

*Red River Review* "At Last I Can Start Suffering"

*Sheila-Na-Gig* "The Myth of Lost Fortune"

*Slant* "The Lady with the Dog"

*Slipstream* "RIPJAKE"

*Song of the San Joaquin* "Attachment," "The Sensitive Poet," "The World's Best Sonnets"

*Syndic Literary Journal* "Gongoozling"

*Torrid Literature Journal* "What I Enjoyed"

*The Twin Bill* "Can't You See It?" and "The Ultimate Penultimate"

*Trampset* "Michigan Bankroll"

*U.S. 1 Worksheets* "Bay State Road Blues"

*Verse Virtual* "How Joe McElroy Met His Wife," Wheel of Fortune"

*Waterways* "Animal Reactions," "No Justice, No Peace"

*Why NICHt?* "Existentialism"

# Contents

Glad All Over

"Happiness is when what you think, what you say, and what you do are in harmony."

—Mahatma Gandhi


This book is for Abby, closer than the vein in my throat, as the Quran has it, especially over this past pandemic time.

# An Expert in the Field of Happiness

*"Happiness is the meaning and the purpose of life, the whole aim and end of human existence."*

—Aristotle

The public radio program promo
announced tomorrow's guest,
"an expert in the field of Happiness."

Who knew happiness was a field
and that there are experts?
People with degrees from prestigious universities
establishing their expertise in being happy?

I have a Master's in English and American Literature and
Language,
another in Publications Design with a Specialization in Creative
Writing,
a Bachelor's in Philosophy
and a certificate from a Computer Programming school.
But I am no expert in Happiness.

I am reasonably content,
a solid thirty-year marriage,
two wonderful daughters,
friends and family for which I am grateful,
comfortable financially,
my health OK for a sexagenarian.
But an expert in Happiness?
Are you kidding?

The Smell of Chlorine

# Celebrity

"I taught Oprah how to swim,"
Eddie's modest reminiscence
more bemused than boastful.
I'd just entered the locker room
from the pool at the Downtown Athletic Club,
standing in a puddle
in front of my locker,
fumbling with the combination lock.

Why not?  Baltimore's a small town.
Eddie knew Winfrey before
she made or broke bestselling writers,
decorated the front covers
of *People* and grocery store tabloids,
elected presidents.

The best I could say,
I knew a guy in high school
back in rural Michigan,
who later became
a studio musician, played
on one of Mick Jagger's solo albums.
My daughter went to high school
with a girl who came in sixth
on *So You Think You Can Dance?*

Fame clings close
when you get next to it,
like the smell of chlorine
on the skin
after the swimming pool.

# Famous

"I was just seventeen,
in the Navy on shore leave,"
Bill reminisced, running the razor
around my ears,
"and Streisand was still a nobody.

"We were at the Bon Soir Club in the Village.
My buddies couldn't stand her,
though I'd raved.
They walked out, shaking their heads,
to meet some girls at the USO."

Streisand had the spotlight shone on Bill
after his friends walked out.
"'Hey, Sailor,'" Bill imitated
Streisand's Brooklyn accent,
as if he had a mouthful of bubblegum,
posing with an insouciant hand on his hip,
"'where your friends goin'?'"

"'And you ain't got a date?'
she demanded. 'Come on up here.'"

Streisand sat in Bill's lap,
crooned "I Want To Be Bad"
into his adolescent ear.

Years later, after she was famous
and Bill a hair stylist in Manhattan,
he designed a wig for Streisand,
in New York filming scenes
for *The Way We Were.*

"That scene where she meets Redford
in the bar, and he's drunk?
That's my wig she's got on.
My claim to fame."

# Meeting of the Titans

When by chance he encountered his idol
on the airplane, both taking the same flight,
Randall Jarrell was like a kid at the stadium,
autograph book in hand.

The legendary quarterback of the Baltimore Colts,
champion of the Greatest Game Ever Played,
about whom Jarrell rhapsodized to his classes—
Jarrell, winner of The National Book Award
for *The Woman at the Washington Zoo,*
Consultant in Poetry at the Library in Congress
(what was later renamed Poet Laureate of the United States),
recipient of a Guggenheim Fellowship,
lecturer in the Princeton Seminars in Literary Criticism,
author of a couple of dozen books
(only about half a dozen when they met)—
Number Nineteen had never heard of Jarrell.
A crushing disappointment.

But then, as Jarrell himself noted—
he who suffered from depression and would later
fling himself in front of a speeding car,
though never technically labeled a suicide—
people do not understand poets or poetry.

"Take Johnny Unitas," he remarked,
by way of illustration,
"Only a few people up in the stands
understand what he is doing.
Most of them have seen only a few games,
they couldn't hope to understand
what is going on."

Still, wouldn't it have been something
had Johnny U. recognized greatness
when it approached him on an airplane?

# River of No Return

That August Sunday in 1962
my father's former student, Vern Baker,
a sometime minor league pitcher,
sprang for tickets to a doubleheader in Detroit,
the Tigers versus the Twins,
all the way across the state from Potawatomi Rapids.
Heaven to a ten-year-old boy.

The Tigers and Twins split the games,
Detroit losing the first in extra innings,
but Dick McAuliffe's homerun
and Al Kaline's RBI double
provided enough to win the second,
Jim Bunning getting the save.
Kaline and Rocky Colavito homered in the first game,
as did Harmon Killebrew for the Twins.
*Magic!*
Vern even knew some of the players;
I got an autograph from Don Mossi.

Afterward, in the magic glow of the day,
we stopped at a filling station for gas
for the long trip back home,
and heard on a transistor radio
Marilyn Monroe was dead.
Even though I was only ten,
I'd have given anything to trade places
with Tommy Rettig, that child actor in *River of No Return*.
Like a flame blown out,
the day had suddenly lost its magic.

# Paw Paw Charlie

The baseball season lasts forever.
I only seem to notice Opening Day,
the playoffs, the World Series:
the beginning and the end.

But as a kid in Michigan
I followed the Tigers' every pitch.
My original hero? Charlie Maxwell,
left-handed, just like me. Same name.

George Kell, who did the radio play-by-play,
called him "Paw Paw Charlie" in his Georgia drawl,
after Maxwell's Michigan hometown,
just sixty miles to the west of mine.

Paw Paw Charlie's peak years
coincided with mine as a hero-worshipper,
between six and ten years old.
He made the All-Star team in 1956,
hit thirty-one homeruns in 1959,
a dozen of them on Sundays,
earning him another nickname, "Sunday Charlie."

But in 1961 the Tigers traded
Harvey Kuenn for Rocky Colavito,
who replaced Paw Paw Charlie in left:
relegated to pinch-hitting,
his days as a Tiger were numbered.

The Tigers won 101 games that season
but still finished eight games behind the Yankees,
after years in the middle of the pack,
where they'd end the following season, too.

I kept track of Paw Paw Charlie
when they traded him to the White Sox in 1962,
but by then he'd passed his prime.
And after he was released by Chicago in 1964?
Went back to Paw Paw to sell automobile parts.
By then I was idolizing rock stars—
Beatles, Animals, Dave Clark Five.

# The Ultimate Penultimate

My friend from work, Terry,
likewise a technical writer,
went with me to the penultimate
Orioles baseball game at Memorial Stadium,
October 5, 1991.

The company'd laid me off
four months before,
the documentation department slimming down
for budgetary reasons.
But I'd found a new job
writing computer procedures
at a local insurance company.

A crisp Indian summer day,
blue skies, autumnal shirtsleeve weather,
we sat in centerfield seats,
plastic cups of draft beer in hand,
watched the final Orioles victory
at the old stadium where they'd played
since moving to town from St. Louis in 1954.
They'd already lost 94 games that season,
would lose to Detroit again the next day.

We also saw the last home run there,
Chito Martinez' two-run shot in the sixth
to give Baltimore the lead they wouldn't lose.

The next day would also be full of lasts:
"I Was There" pennants on sale,
a parade of heroes from the past,
Mike Flanagan pitching the ninth inning,
Baltimore's last Cy Young Award winner (1979).

But Terry and I saw the good parts.

It was also the last time I ever saw Terry,
he and his family leaving Baltimore the next year
for another job in St. Louis.

# Can't You See It?

I couldn't get a ticket that night—
sold out long ago—
and besides, I had to go to work next day,
drive my kids to their grade school,
the new academic year having just begun.

A hot summer day, the temperature topping 90,
barely cooling when the sun went down,
a festive gaiety filled the city.
The O's hadn't been a contender for years,
the glory days of the 1970's
a quarter century in the rearview mirror.

But tonight the city would celebrate:
Cal Ripken, the Iron Man,
would play his 2,131$^{st}$ consecutive game,
passing Lou Gehrig on the all-time list.

The Orioles beat the Angels 4—2,
behind Mike Mussina's pitching,
Ripken going two for four with an RBI.

But best of all?
Joan Jett sang the National Anthem,
the Camden Yards crowd heaving up
a thunderous "Oh!"
when Joan got to "Oh, say can you see…"

Like the kids who claimed
they'd gone to Woodstock,
I'd always boast I'd seen the game,
telling the lie and feeling no shame.

# Go, Cubs!

Danny'd spent his entire life rooting for the Cubs.
As a kid he'd go to Wrigley, cheer
for a succession of heroes from Ernie Banks
to Ryne Sandberg to Sammy Sosa.
Over and over they'd broken his heart,
losing the NLCS to the Padres, then the Giants,
and the heartbreaker in 2003 to the Marlins
when the kid in the stands
disrupted a catch by Moisés Alou
in the sixth game at Wrigley,
the Cubs leading the series three games to two,
four outs away from the World Series.

But hey, if Bob Dylan could win the Nobel Prize,
why couldn't the Cubs win the World Series this time?
But Danny'd given up hope,
his Cubbies down three games to two,
headed back to Cleveland for the final games—
even though Lebron had faced the same odds,
winning the NBA title for the Cavs
just a few months before.

When Chicago blew a three-run lead in the eighth,
four outs away from victory,
Danny, who'd allowed himself to hope again,
felt as if the gods were laughing at him,
twisting the knife.  Only, *Mirabile Dictu!*
The Cubs won the Series in extra innings!
November 2, 2016!

But a week later,
Danny's elation would evaporate like mist
when he woke to the presidential election results,
another improbable outcome.

# Love

In London for a semester abroad
her junior year in college,
my daughter sprang for tickets
to opening day at Wimbledon
for my sixtieth birthday.

The Baltimore City Public Schools
girls' singles tennis champion
only four years before,
Zoe and I shared an admiration for Roger Federer,
determined we'd see him play a match.

Staying at a Holiday Inn on the High Street, Colliers Wood,
a quarter of an hour from the tennis courts,
we left a call for a taxi for four in the morning,
got to the site, sat for hours on dew-drenched grass,
as if at Woodstock, 1969, people in pup tents,
sleeping bags and air mattresses,
while we only had our jackets against the chill,
watching the sun come up in the east.

But it paid off!
After endless hours weaving in a line to the turnstiles,
we took our seats in No. 1 Court.
We'd see the reigning champ, Djokovic,
on Centre Court two days later,
but Federer was god-like, sublime,
taking apart Albert Ramos 6—1, 6—1, 6—1,
finishing with a love game,
an ace down the center on match point.

The hour-long tube ride
from Wimbledon to Heathrow and home
felt like a victory lap.

# In the Clearing Stands a Boxer

Only fifteen when he became
Middleweight Champion of Greece—
All-Balkans Middleweight Champ the following year—
Salamo Arouch, "The Ballet Dancer,"
had never lost a fight
when the Nazis deported his family,
along with 60,000 other Jews,
from Thessaloniki to Auschwitz.

The Nazis killed his parents,
his three younger sisters,
almost the minute
they got out of the cattle car,
but when they learned Salamo was a boxer,
they spared him for their entertainment,
their gambling pleasure.

Two or three times a week
The Ballet Dancer got into the ring,
fighting for his life over 200 times,
the losers sent to the gas chambers or shot.

Undefeated at Auschwitz—
though he'd had to fight twice
while recovering from dysentery—
Salamo was sent next to Bergen-Belsen,
liberated in April 1945,
still standing, if bloodied, scarred,
after the final bell,
but you can bet he'd carry the reminders
in his anger and his shame
until the day he died in 2009.

# Denkmal

More bemused than outraged
when fans of Michael Jackson took over
the 1862 monument to Orlando di Lasso,
the medieval Belgian composer,
on Munich's Promenadeplatz—
in front of the Hotel Bayerischer Hof,
where "Jacko" used to stay—
as a memorial to the pop star
after his death ten years before,
Adele nevertheless lamented Orlando's neglect.

But after the latest accusations of child abuse,
Michael's  music banned from European airwaves,
Adele was disturbed by the hatred she heard,
the sarcastic arguments back and forth.

"Let's destroy the statues of Wagner—
the anti-Semite—too, and
Benjamin Britten and Oscar Wilde,
with tastes similar to Jackson's,"
one man sneered.
"Even Beethoven, the misanthrope.
After all, art is only worthwhile
when the artist is a decent human being!"

"Michael Jackson, an artist?
He was merely an entertainer!"

"Art's not supposed to be entertaining?"

Adele shook her head.
She'd always admired Orlando di Lasso,
remembering now his *Lagrime di San Pietro*.
The tears of Saint Peter.

31

# Alexander Pushkin Dies in a Duel

How would *you* react
to an anonymous lampoon
awarding you the title,
*Deputy Grand Master of the Order of Cuckolds?*

We were sure it was the work of Baron d'Anthès.
He'd been sniffing around Pushkin's wife
in Saint Petersburg society,
but to my knowledge,
the beautiful Natalia'd rejected him.

Married six years, four children,
Pushkin was as certain of her fidelity
as he was of d'Anthès's mischief.

Surc, tongues wagged as they always will
when a stunning beauty's involved—
some called Natalia Russia's Helen of Troy,
and no denying she *was* a flirt.
She had so many admirers.

But the mock letter couldn't be ignored,
and even though the Baron denied writing it—
and face it, it wasn't exactly *Eugene Onegin*—
the week after d'Anthès's marriage
to Natalia's sister Yekaterina,
the two of them met at Chernaya Rekha
on the outskirts of Saint Petersburg,
a cold day at the end of January.

# The Plot Against America

That semester at the community college,
we taught Philip Roth's *The Plot Against America*
in our Intro to Literature classes.
Mina and I shared an office,
both of us adjuncts in the English Department.

She told me she'd compared the novel,
in which Charles Lindbergh, a Nazi
sympathizer, is elected president,
to the Trump administration:
the persecution of minorities
(Jews instead of immigrants and Muslims),
the attacks on the free press,
an authoritarian con man in the Oval Office.
Her students, unable or unwilling
to see the similarities, thought
she just had an ax to grind,
still hadn't gotten over the election.

I remembered Professor Wilson,
my Elizabethan Lit. professor
when I was a college student,
talking about all the sex symbols
in Spenser and Shakespeare.
Billy Dooley, in the desk next to mine,
wondered in whisper if Wilson wasn't
getting any sex at home.

"They don't think Trump's 'presidential,'"
Mina clarified, "but
they aren't scared out of their wits, either."

Pulsing like a Migraine on the Dashboard

# Snow Day

My second grade daughter's book report
about Rachel Carson is due today.
We talked about DDT and *Silent Spring*
last night after supper,
before the freezing rain started to fall.

In the morning the sidewalks are ice rinks,
and the school is closed for the day.
I call work to say I'll be late.
I have deadlines to meet,
but what can I do?

Sipping a mug of hot coffee,
I listen to the radio rattle
the names of the schools closing for the day,
like some Day of Atonement drama
in which names are inscribed in the Book of Life.
Outside I hear a crash,
the sound of the Apocalypse.

A young guy with an earring
erupts from a red Camaro,
already gesturing his innocence,
blaming it all on Nature.
The Camaro's right bumper is wedged
up under the trunk of my next door neighbor's Saturn
like a stray dog trying to mate with a pedigreed pup.

The Camaro caromed off one parked car
and then another, like a guy in a singles' bar
hitting on chicks

before finally sticking its face
into Susan's Saturn's nether regions,
a tongue of exhaust fumes
licking the frigid air.

Already I can hear the stories
I'll be telling over and over again
when I finally get in to work,
probably not until tomorrow,
I concede with sneaky relief.

# Low Cool

"Did you open it?"
Glen cut through my attempt at small talk,
focusing on the task at hand.
I'd discovered his garage through a friend:
an honest, competent mechanic.

"No, I wasn't actually sure
where the coolant was supposed to go,"
I confessed, immediately wishing
I'd kept my mouth shut,
Glen's disdain eloquent in his silence.

The evening before,
my dashboard had lit up
like a terrorist bomb,
a bell dinging, insistent, relentless as a migraine,
warning something horrible was about to happen.
A little square box with a squiggly line
pulsed on the dashboard panel
like a third-degree burn—
no telling what it meant,
some engineer's idea of a symbol,
hieroglyph-incomprehensible.

Glen twisted the top off the container—
inside bone dry. He poured in
the viscous green liquid,
life-giving elixir, sealed the top,
waving away my offer of pay.
I felt ineffectual driving away.
What could I do for him in return?
Describe the rhyme scheme of a Petrarchan sonnet?

# Failure

I'd graduated from the university in May,
a degree in English,
and here it was October
and I was still delivering pizzas.

"Well, at least she's not
going to marry him,"
I overheard Katie's mom
saying to her husband
when their daughter moved in with me,
just three weeks ago.

At least I drove my own VW
and didn't wear a silly uniform
like my co-workers back
in that greasy pizzeria,
even if I had to pay for my own gas.

The cops stopped me
when I was driving up to the dorm
to deliver a pepperoni pizza and mozzarella sticks
a group of coeds'd ordered.

The whole area was in lockdown.
"Some kid jumped off the tenth floor,"
the one with the stripes on his shoulders told me.
"Apparently he got a bad grade on a Chemistry exam,
said his parents would kill him."

# The Grifter

"Excuse me." The pretty girl
in the peasant blouse leaned
over the hood of my car
as I fiddled with the lock.
I'd just stopped at the Welcome Center
across the Pennsylvania state line
to get a map and use the restroom.
"Is Pittsburgh three hours north?"

What a gorgeous woman, I thought,
her blouse loose, leaning toward me,
and I had a momentary fantasy,
a tryst in an interstate motel.
"Yes, it is. Take the Turnpike at Breezewood."

"Can you give me a ride?"
The motel room fantasy downshifted
to a desolate side road,
a furtive blow job in a parked car.

"I'm kind of running late,"
I improvised. She did not appear
desperate. This was her lifestyle.
I was her prey.
"Headed for Ohio."

"Can you take me
to the next town, then?"
She leaned closer, her blouse
opened to a further promise.

"I really don't think—" I stammered;
realizing this was not an argument
I could win,

I climbed into the car,
shrugged, apologetic,
but she had already turned
to the older couple
approaching their Plymouth Voyager.

# Collision

Pulling out of a parking space at the mall
I nearly ram a boatlike Buick
creeping up behind me.

The driver rolls down
her window,
bleats like a beaten sheep.
"You hit me!"

We get out of our cars,
medieval combatants meeting on the field,
to examine her fenders.
Nothing.  Not even a scratch.

Strands of limp white hair
wave across her pale forehead
like antennae in the breeze,
her pale eyes tired with worry.
"My husband will kill me
if I come home with a dent."

I run my hand along the door,
over the hood,
as if soothing a nervous horse,
invite her to touch the Buick, too,
verify there isn't a mark.

"He's dying," she cries then,
her face crumpling into its wrinkles
like a trunk collapsing in a rear-ender.
"This will be his last Christmas."

# Denting My Self-Esteem

The rusty old Cadillac
sat angled over the slanting lines
in the grocery store parking lot
like the wrong jigsaw puzzle piece.
Backing out, I caught the rear fender,
yanking away the chrome wing.

"Yes, you did!"
The righteous old lady
in the Ford Escort on my other side
shook her finger at me
like a reproving schoolmarm
when I got out of my car
to examine the damage.

*But look at the cockeyed way*
*the car's parked in that space!*
*As much the owner's fault as mine!*

"Well, what can I do?
I can't wait here all day
for the owner to show up,"
I objected, my dim view of the owner,
the eyesore that was the car,
the careless way it had been parked,
all evident in the high whine of my voice.

"You can leave your name and number
and the name of your insurance company
on a piece of paper," she spat,
chiding a disobedient student.

She got into her car
as I fumbled for a pen in the glovebox.
When she'd gone,
I tore up the note,
drove away, looking all around for witnesses,
a truant late for class.

# A Whole New Gestalt

Leaving the grocery store parking lot,
I try to ignore the woman
waving at me beside my car,
hoping the light will change,
but she taps on the glass,
and I can no longer pretend.

I roll down the window,
already reaching for my wallet,
when she asks me for a ride.
An Indian woman, she speaks
in the cultured accent of a character
from an Ivory-Merchant film on Masterpiece Theater,
and though I remember the last time
a strange woman asked me for a lift—
a black girl with an infant on her hip
who offered a blow job for ten dollars
as soon as she climbed into the car—
I pop open the passenger door,
only then noticing the two large bags of groceries.

The address she gives is ten blocks away,
impossible to walk on such a hot summer day,
but I tell her she is brave
to ask for a ride from a complete stranger.
Some years our city
has the highest murder rate in the nation;
drug mules coming up the coast from Miami
routinely killed in turf wars.

"Oh, I could tell you were harmless,"
she laughs in that musical sing-song,
waving her hand as if shooing a flea,
and though I take this as a compliment,
I can see the benign older guy she must see,
the one who has just learned his daughter
 is pregnant with his first grandchild.

# Backseat Blues

I hated the way Nick always made me
sit in back with the posse
while he sat up front like a prince,
Wayne his chauffeur.

"Don't worry, you're my girl,"
he'd coo, when we were alone,
usually in my bedroom
when my mom and dad were out,
Nick not having a car of his own.

Another Friday night with his pals,
me, Chuck and Mikey in the back,
Nick up front blowing smoke rings at the windshield,
twisting the radio dial,
playing drums on the dashboard.
I could see the fantasy in his head:
drummer for some rock group,
girls dying to be with him.

That's when I noticed Chuck,
sipping his beer beside me,
eyeing my tits with a sidelong glance,
thinking I wouldn't notice.

I put my hand on his leg, as if by accident,
left it there, scooched ever so slightly closer,
so Mikey wouldn't even notice.

Chuck got the idea.
It wasn't five minutes before
he'd tugged my blouse out of my pants,
slid his hand like a snake,
up the front of my body.

I won't deny it felt good,
the way he stroked my breasts,
as if pet cats, squeezed, gentle
as only a lovesick boy can be,
but it was getting even with Nick
that really turned me on.

# The Rusty Studebaker

We piled into Wayne's four-door, underage
high schoolers, six-packs of Pabst in hand,
Winstons tucked into shirt pockets.
Friday night, party time.

Wayne drove out 29-Mile Road,
parked behind a stand of trees,
killed the engine, left the radio on.
Sam the Sham, "Wooly Bully."

Wayne bought the car with money he earned at the A&P,
packing groceries, pushing carts to the lot,
loading housewives' trunks,
"Yes ma'am," and "Thank-you ma'am."

But Nick was the leader; he sat shotgun,
the place of honor,
while his girlfriend Kelly,
relegated to the backseat,
sat between me and Mikey.

That's how I came to sneak my hand
up under her shirt, hidden by the darkness.
She put her hand on my thigh;
I took it for a sign,
probably getting even with Nick,
though I didn't put two and two together at the time,
just basked in my good fortune.
"You've Lost that Lovin' Feelin'"
fading to "Mrs. Brown You've Got a Lovely Daughter,"
while I twirled Kelly's nipples
between forefinger and thumb,
my lust thick as a swamp.

But where could it go from there,
trapped in the back seat,
"For Your Love" melting into "Red Roses for a Blue Lady,"
while Wayne, Mikey and Nick talked baseball.
*The heft in my hand, the softness of her flesh.*

We finished our beers; Wayne started the car;
Kelly pushed my hand away;
we drove home.
I groaned all night.

# Did That Just Happen?

"Hey, old man!"

The taunt whizzed over my shoulder,
a bullet that nevertheless hit its mark.
Turning my head, I saw
a blur of red flesh and chin stubble
swing into my vision
like some funhouse scare puppet.

"Yeah, you.
What the fuck you doing,
slamming my car like that?"

"What are you talking about?"

"*What are you talking about?*"
the kid mimicked, a prissy voice.
"Are your ears as useless as your balls?"

"Dean!" a girl's voice squealed.
We both turned to the blond beach chick.

Dean's eyes lit up.
I was already yesterday's news.
Like a puppy he trotted over
to the girl in tanktop and shorts,
his tail wagging.

# The Crud

My mother called him "The Crud,"
my brother's friend Alan.
I'm not sure what she had against him,
besides his lack of ambition—
she a schoolteacher, after all—
Alan destined to work
in one of the steel factories
after graduating from high school—
at least until the steel factories all closed.

The Crud loved cars.
He could tell you the make and model and year
of anything with four wheels and an engine,
sported decals of hotrods and muscle cars
all over his school folders.

He did speak vaguely
of "joining the service,"
as his older brother had,
then having all his teeth pulled,
dentures installed in their place,
the stubby twisted teeth in his mouth,
a source of private anguish.

When my brother mentioned to their friends
our mother called Alan "The Crud,"
the nickname stuck,
but only behind his back.
Everybody referred to Alan as "The Crud."
Initially offended, hurt, Alan soon embraced it,
wore the sobriquet like a badge,
though still, nobody called him
"Crud" to his face.

Sometimes I wish I knew
what became of The Crud
after I left home,
but never enough to try to find out.

# Poker Faces

When I finally returned to Potawatomi Rapids
after years living overseas,
in the foreign service,
one embassy after another,
I was horrified to learn
the horny old goat Brent Robinson
pursued my niece Beverly
like an animal in heat,
a woman thirty years younger than he.

"Robinson's a shrewd banker,"
Uncle Pete, Bev's grandfather, observed,
when the local rich man's name
came up in conversation.
He had some sort of power over Pete,
maybe a loan of some kind
on Uncle Pete's car dealership.

"And how does he plan
to get Bev to marry him?"
I asked, trying to keep my voice neutral,
a guy in a poker  game,
cagey about his hand.

Uncle Pete smiled
like the guy holding the royal flush
in a game without wild cards.

"Only if she accepts his proposal,"
he laughed, his eyes crinkling
in a way that made me miss
all those years apart from my family.
"And I don't think
that's happening any time soon."

# No Justice, No Peace

Two days after the Freddie Gray riot,
I come off the expressway at 28th Street,
slow down for the light at Sisson.
A white van veers into my lane,
into my car.

The Rolling Stones are on the CD player,
a cover of a Smokey Robinson song.
*It was just my imagination runnin' away with me.*

I get out, circle to the front.
The other driver, a grizzled Black man,
looks scared, waves his hand
to suggest no harm's been done.
His passenger, also African-American,
stares at me, wide-eyed and sober,
as if I were the southern highway patrol.
*It was just my imagination runnin' away with me.*

 "I seen it happen," the guy with the Homeless sign
standing at the intersection declares.
"I seen the accident."
We ignore him, but I wonder
whose side he'd take, Black himself.
*It was just my imagination runnin' away with me.*

I don't see any damage.
We return to our cars
without exchanging insurance information.
My car seems to drive just fine.

Only when I get home,
try to open the passenger side door
to recover my belongings, and can't,
do I see the damage to the hinge, low down.
The whole door will have to be replaced.
*It was just my imagination runnin' away with me.*

# Driving While Black

OJ's dog Hoops' blue eyes burned
a cold arctic rage,
as if promising eternal torment,
in a face the ghost-white of an opossum;
made me nervous the first time I saw him,
even if he was essentially a gentle animal.

Driving into the glare of the sun,
OJ told me, he missed the traffic light sliding
from yellow to red, and right away
the *gotcha* whoop of a police siren
brought him to a stop.

"License, registration," the cop demanded
when OJ rolled down the window.

Fumbling in the glove box,
OJ mentioned the blinding glare.
He'd been on his way to the dog park
to give Hoops his morning run.
As if on cue, Hoops poked his face
out of the rolled-down window.

"What kind of a dog is that?"
the officer asked, wary of this Hound of the Baskervilles.
He handed back OJ's papers,
considering the blue-eyed dog.

"Part Alaskan husky, part Boxer," OJ answered.
"Some other breeds, too."

"Just a warning." The cop pushed away from the window,
patting Hoops' nose, rubbing an ear.
"Yeah, that sun *is* blinding, isn't it?"

"It was having a blue-eyed blond that saved me,"
OJ told me later, laughing.
"I couldn't be a complete criminal, could I?"

# Attachment

Though I always rolled my eyes
at people who named their cars,
anthropomorphizing them the way, as kids,
my brother and I did our hamsters,

I took to calling my Chevy Malibu "Spots"
because of the bird poop all over the fenders and hood
from where I parked under the maple tree
behind our house,
referring to Spots as I might a pet.

I drove that car a dozen years
before I finally had to trade it in
after somebody sideswiped me
and the repair was more expensive
than the car was worth.

But when I traded it in,
I felt a sharp pang of nostalgia
for this car that had conveyed me to work,
vacations, errands, meetings all those years,
the car in which my kids learned to drive,
as if it contained a whole era of my life,
represented an irretrievable passage of time.

I got a two-hundred-dollar trade-in
and drove away in a used Nissan Sentra,
leaving Spots to be sold for parts.

# Trumplandia

We sailed into the Birch Run exit
like a leaky catamaran,
the *Service Engine Now* light
pulsing like a migraine on the dashboard.

After checking into a motel,
calling Triple-A as if tossing out a lifeline,
locating likely local repair shops—
Sunday afternoon, all businesses closed—

we went to dinner
at Oscar and Joey's Roadhouse,
a nearby bar, trophy kills—deer,
elk, moose—mounted on the walls.

"Went into limp mode," the guy
at the table next to us nodded
when we told him about our car problems.
He named a garage we could try.

"A Nissan?" he frowned, disapproving.
"Used to work at GM in Flint
until they shut down the plant
more'n fifteen years ago now.

"Now I drive down to Chrysler
in Detroit, every day,
a hundred and six miles there,
a hundred and six miles back.

"Why don't I move?
I just ain't a city boy.
'Sides, I got my farm up here.
Okay, sorry about you folks' car."

When he got up, he pointed
to the stuffed bear next to the bar,
rearing up on its hind legs,
Canadian flags behind its ears.

"Missy shot that up in Canada,"
he indicated the waitress with a jerk of his head.
"She says the best part was
her husband didn't shoot nothin'."

# The Kindness of Strangers

"A torque converter clutch fault,"
the garage mechanic told us,
and by the sound of the words,
I knew it was going to be expensive.

"Trouble is we can't do nothing about it,"
he went on, "since it's a Nissan,
and we only work on GM products.
"But let me call up to Saginaw."
He picked up the phone.
"See if I can't find someone to help."

On our way home to Maryland
from our family vacation,
our car had broken down,
about eighty miles north of Ann Arbor.
Now we had to improvise.

I remembered my father
downshifting into *Aw shucks* gear
to converse with blue collar types,
a college professor himself,
not a snob but afraid of appearing superior,
as if getting your hands dirty
were somebody else's problem.

# Michigan Bankroll

"We called it a 'Brooklyn roll,'"
my friend Bob, who grew up in Flatbush,
tells me, "channeling the B-movie gangsters,"
when I mention the guy we ran into
on his way to the Indian casino near Battle Creek,
white shoes, white belt girding
a bulging middle-aged tummy,
hair in a careful combover,
sporting a roll of bills,
a Benjamin on top of a lump of ones and fives.

We were on our way north
after visiting my disabled mother
in the smalltown where I grew up,
in the house she'd lived in for sixty-five years,
the last twenty as a widow,
gambling on still living
another few on her own,
the brave face she put on it
like that bankroll the guy flashed,
the big bill on top hiding the frailty.

I came upon the guy at a rest area,
checking himself out in the bathroom mirror;
unasked, he told me where he was going.
I pointed him out to my wife as we drove away,
agreeing he was a real "type."

"A gangster in his own mind,"
I nodded to Bob.

# RIPJAKE

The vanity plate on the car ahead of me—
at first I think it's gotta be a bodybuilder,
vain about his muscles, his abs—"ripped"—
"vanity plates" so aptly named.
But then I wonder if it has something to do
with getting high, a smartass frat boy boasting, maybe.
Or maybe it's some hip new urban slang
I've never heard before.
Riptide. Ripsaw. (Rickshaw?) Ripjake.

Then I see the *In Loving Memory*
decal pasted on the back windshield,
and below it:
Jacob Miller, 6/20/81—9/11/01.
I suddenly feel a little guilty,
a solemnity falling over me like a shroud.
I can't see the driver.
Parent, spouse, sibling, lover, friend?

Fifteen years ago.
Had Jake been at the Pentagon?
Barely twenty years old;
he could have been a solider.
World Trade Center towers?
Unlucky passenger on an airplane headed west?

Or was the date just a coincidence?
Others died that day, too—
cancer, car wrecks, gunshots, heart failure.

The car turns left at the next light,
and I go on.
Rest in Peace.

# Freitod

"As beautiful as an electric chair." Jo Nesbo, *Nemesis*

I'd just pulled off the highway,
ravenous as a wolf after a day
of sales meeting and miles in the car,
greeted by a strip of gas stations,
fast food franchises, making me think
of the midway at a carnival—
games, rides, freakshows announced
by flashing neon, bright primary-colored signs.

I pulled in to a Chick-fil-A,
the most convenient drive-in on my right
with a stoplight to make the departure easier.
I knew about Chick-fil-A's political agenda,
disapproval of same-sex marriage, LGBT rights,
but food is food is expedience.

As if in punishment, though,
I ran into Family Night,
a couple of single mothers
and a passel of kids
that made me think of a litter of puppies,
ketchup smeared across their faces,
jamming Chick-n-strips into their mouths
as if they were racing a timer.

"Sonny ain't paid no child support
for three-five months," the heavy mother complained,
more depleted than angry, her cheeks
sliding down her face like melted plastic.

"He ain't got no job," the skinny one pointed out,
an African-American girl whose collarbones
stood out like a steering wheel.
"Hey, Lonzo! Quit messin' around!"
she called at one of the kids.

Suddenly I wasn't hungry,
but I ordered a grilled chicken sandwich to go,
and the traffic light?
Turned green when I drove up to the intersection,
a smooth left putting me back on the highway,
a hundred miles from home.

# Road Rage

A blond woman behind the wheel
of a four-wheel drive weapon
squeezes in front of me going seventy-five mph,
in a hurry to get to wherever she's going.
I hit the brakes.
My daughter in the carseat jerks forward.
A car behind me honks a warning;
we are geese flying north.

How I wish the fall of a sparrow
were controlled by some governing intelligence.
How I wish some watchful benevolent god
looked lovingly after us all,
ensuring safety, a certain arrival.

How I wish I had a gun.

# The World's Best Sonnets

Driving to Cape May, New Jersey,
in the distance we saw the water tower,
block letters making a bold civic claim.

I thought of smalltown pride,
the bogus inflated contentions—
"Home of the original boy scout troop",
"Birthplace of Mother's Day",
"Soybean Capital of the World",
"World's Largest Pinecone".

"What's that say?" I asked Abby,
our eyesight not as sharp
as it was when we were younger.

"The World's Best Sonnets?" she speculated,
squinting at the letters,
not believing her eyes.
Where were we, anyway?
 Stratford-upon-Avon?

"Home of the World's Best Sunsets,"
we said at the same time,
as we got closer.
Mystery solved.

# Full Service

"Oh, right. They pump your gas for you
in the state of New Jersey," I reflected.
We'd just pulled into an Exxon
on our way to Cape May for the weekend.
In an era of self-service automation—
self-checkout grocery scanners,
ATMs instead of bank tellers doling out the dollars—
this rule you couldn't pump your own gas
seemed quaint and anachronistic,
and I even felt like a hostage,
our departure dependent on the whim of this kid,
when he'd take our money,
when he'd bring us our change,

and I remembered my old man,
thirty-five years ago back in Michigan,
pulling up at a pump and being told
he had to fill his own gas tank.

"Piss on this," he'd muttered, incensed.
"I'm not going to do their work for them."
Even though I offered to get out and do it myself,
he drove away in a pique;
we circled the town another half an hour
until we found a service station
with a boy who did it for us.
He even checked the oil,
wiped the windshield.
My father drove away, happy.

Loss Is Such a Potent Lure

# Romance

My father told the tale
of pursuing my mom for weeks,
even after she said no five or six times,
when he asked her out on a date.
It sounded so romantic,
his persistence in the face of rejection.
*True love conquers all.*
Dad taught English at the Community College,
Mom was the department secretary.

But when I tried the same thing
with Suzanne at the office—
we work in a big insurance company—
I was called to the manager's office for harassment,
accused of contributing to an intimidating,
hostile working environment,
made to watch workplace behavior videos,
placed on administrative leave.

Mostly I wonder about the story
I'll tell my children one day.

# Destiny Foretold

"When I was young I wrote song lyrics
I knew nobody would ever sing," he told her,
and he caroled: *Somewhere in my mind*
*There's a man who can't get to sleep.*
*He's got his eyes wide open*
*and his concentration's running deep.*
*He's been up all night*
*digging dirt in a diamond mine.*
*Somewhere in my mind*
*I'm thinking of you all the time.*

"The diamond mine image was supposed to convey
the idea of a guy burrowing endlessly
into the fertile soil of his soul," he explained,
"relentless as a worker ant.
I can't shake the feeling
the song is about you."

"But you wrote it about somebody else, right?"

"Yeah, but I've forgotten who."

# Breaking My Heart

"Don't go breakin' my heart,"
Elton John sings to Kiki Dee.
And what a funny metaphor for emotions,
I think, the heart. Why the heart?
All that love and hurt and betrayal and jealousy,
all that longing and desire, all that
passion, sentiment, whatever else.

And that funny red balloon shape,
where did that come from?
Silphium, a possible contraceptive,
represented in that shape, 6$^{th}$ century BCE,
carrots, with their estrogenic properties.
The red scallop with the dent in the base,
the point a stabbing downward dagger,
early fourteenth century, though
the heart as symbol of romantic love
even earlier, 1250, only then
it looked more like a pine cone.

The heart we all know from Valentine's Day,
the one on playing cards
since late fifteenth century,
like a spread vulva, buttocks, the pubic mound:
isn't that the one that breaks?
The one that gets pierced by Cupid's arrow?
Cupid—from the Latin for "desire":
He didn't actually shoot for the heart.
Any direct hit would do.

"I won't go breakin' your heart,"
Kiki sings back to Elton.

# The Myth of Lost Fortune

Loss is such a potent lure anyway—
love, money, family, fame—
the thing you had
but not long enough to appreciate—
popularity, a profession, innocence
(happiness, harmony)—
the thing you spend the rest of your life
trying to recover.

Sometimes life seems nothing
but a series of losses.
It's always there, waiting.
Death—yours or someone else's.

I had it once.
Or did I only *think* I had it?
Wish-fulfillment in its purest form?

Recovery's the key, the missing piece
that completes the puzzle:
not the piece recovered,
the key that unlocks the loss.

It's here, somewhere.
Buried. Hidden.
Not irretrievable, even though
you'll never find it.
Maybe there never was
a treasure after all.
But one day, you know
you'll find it.

# Maskenfreiheit

"You're not hiding anything
with that character 'Joni'
in your novel.
Anybody can see
it's you you're writing about,
you and your shitty marriage."

"Still, it gives me the freedom
to explore my feelings."

"Well, whatever.
I do admire your sex scenes."

"I'm just afraid
my husband is going to divorce me
after he reads it.
He'll be so embarrassed."

"That's what I meant."

# Mahlneid

How I longed for what he had,
the fellow perched like a peacock
in the corner booth by the window,
holding hands with the lively woman
whose breasts lay on the table before him
like an offering, a promise,
as she leaned forward, confiding,
unself-conscious, eyes sparkling like jewels,
smile warm, kind, *intimate,*
as if she were somebody
with whom you could share secrets,
and that life-sustaining promise she offered,
that *promise*—

interrupted momentarily by the eggplant fries
the waitress placed before the man,
which, if I'd had my wits about me,
I'd have ordered, too,
instead of this limp lettuce salad.

# Fighting Fair

"If two men are fighting and the wife of one of them comes to rescue her husband from his assailant, and she reaches out and seizes him by his genitals, you shall cut off her hand. Show her no pity."

—Deuteronomy 25:11-12

Even now, decades later,
I think of Jenny on the playground,
kicking her tormentors in the balls
when they tried reaching up her dress,
all of us just hitting puberty, or about to,
sixth-graders on the cusp of junior high,
not really sure what sex was about
or how to go about it,
but excited by it nonetheless.

Mister Watson, the principal,
called Jenny into his office
when Bobby and Rick told on her,
both of them writhing on the ground,
tears in their eyes, squeezing themselves
into a fetal position against the pain.

Too proud to explain her actions,
Jenny spent the next week in detention,
scrubbing the blackboards,
pounding the chalk out of erasers,
sneezing against the dust.

What would I have done
if Mister Watson had asked me
what had really happened?

I wanted to think I'd defend her,
but would I have stuck with my own tribe?
The thought tortured my conscience.
I had a big crush on Jenny,
and had I been bolder,
I might have tried reaching under her skirt, too.

# Pity

"If two men are fighting and the wife of one of them comes to rescue her
husband from his assailant, and she reaches out and seizes him by his
genitals, you shall cut off her hand. Show her no pity."

—Deuteronomy 25:11-12

What a pussy my "boyfriend" Jimmy was!
He liked me because I was tough,
punked out in black leather, mascara,
my thick dark hair a hornets' nest.
He didn't mind the net t-shirts either.

But when that football player Rocky
pushed him into the wall,
snatched the cigarette from his lip
as if brushing away a gnat,
crushed it under his boot
like he was squashing a bug?

Jimmy just stood there
with that Sid Vicious sneer on his face
as if that could intimidate anybody,
a sign of a superiority
only he knew the meaning of,
as if to say, I ain't afraid.
Then Rocky only shoved him again.

So what did I do?
Grabbed that big jerk by the balls,
twisted like I was turning a wrench.
Rocky sank to his knees, whimpering,
tried to swat me away,
feeble as a kitten,
his voice going high with his pain.

But then what did Jimmy do?
Probably thought I showed him up,
so he started saying the only reason
I grabbed Rocky's dick,
was I wanted it for myself—
You want to suck that thing, don't you?—
not to save his skinny little ass.
He acted like I'd done something wrong!

But you know what?
I only pitied him.

# Cutting My Losses

"If two men are fighting and the wife of one of them comes to rescue her husband from his assailant, and she reaches out and seizes him by his genitals, you shall cut off her hand. Show her no pity."
—Deuteronomy 25:11-12

"Is that a roll of quarters
in your pocket,
or are you just glad to see me?"

"What?"
Confusion clouded Rocky's face,
already dim with a kind of perpetual incomprehension.
Besides, he was already distracted,
his arm around my throat in a stranglehold.

Rita had even less patience
for stupidity than I did,
which is how I got into the fight
with Rocky in the first place.
She'd made a disparaging remark
about his intelligence, comparing him
to her neighbor's rheumy-eyed dog,
a slobbering, slow-moving mutt
that smelled like a fetid swamp.
When I laughed,
Rocky came after me.

"*What?*" Rita mimicked Rocky,
making her voice sound so dumb
you could almost see
the knuckles dragging across the floor.
Her hand curled like a hawk's talon,
Rita reached for the bump in his pants,
squeezed as if ringing out a wet rag.

"Yow!" Rocky screamed, releasing me.
I ran. Rita was an admirable girl,
but I knew she wasn't
so good for my health and well-being.

# Periodic Table

Chemistry class was always a bitch
with all those two-letter symbols
for the elements, about a hundred of them,
that we had to spit back on tests—
metals, halogens, gases—
stuff I didn't care about,
since I was planning to major
in Philosophy once I got to college.

But it was the lab experiments
that really freaked me out,
mixing acids, growing crystals,
immersing an LED in liquid nitrogen,
heating mercury thiocyanate
to produce Pharaoh's Serpent.

All thumbs, I always got stuck
with lab partners inept as me,
as if we were the last kids to be picked
in gym class, when choosing sides.

But one time I was teamed with Diane McCall,
sitting hip-to-hip on the high stools
at the heavy granite lab table
deflecting a water stream with a charged rod.
She was wearing some girlie scent,
which excited me, as always.

Our rod happened to be negatively charged,
so it attracted the hydrogen,
bent the stream toward it.

Diane and I looked at each other, shrugged.
Then Diane touched the bump in my pants
where an adolescent erection had sprouted.

"What's that?" she asked with feigned innocence.

# Life Begins

When I found out my niece Cady,
nineteen, was three months pregnant,
it only confirmed what I suspected
from hints she posted on her Facebook page.

But I sure wasn't going to ask.
My sister Etta would have jumped all over me
for getting into her and Cady's business—
the nosy, judgmental older brother.

Mom was the one who told me.
I acted all surprised, of course,
asked who the father was,
how Cady was feeling.

"Jordy's getting a divorce," Mom told me,
matter-of-fact, as if telling me his job.
"His wife has a three-month old baby.
Jordy's a very good man, very sweet."

Sometimes I get the feeling
Mom and Etta bait me,
try to provoke a shrewd observation
they can get all self-righteous about.

Like: Is Cady going to keep the baby?
Is Cady dropping out of college?
Does Cady still want to be a doctor?

# Disapproval

When I turned ten, I started noticing
the sounds my mother and sister made
chewing their food. Utterly revolting!

"Could you please stop making those noises?"
I pled, Joanie rolling her eyes at Mom
as if to say, *Ziggy's being a pain again.*

The slurping, the chewing, sucking.
I'd start to panic
when Mom called us to dinner.

I started wearing headphones at mealtimes,
just so I wouldn't freak out.
Mom called Doctor Goodman.

Misophonia," she pronounced,
giving a name to my aversion.
"Kafka suffered from it, too."

Mom and Joanie looked at each other.
They'd privately assumed I blamed them
for Dad walking out on us the year before.

# The Lady with the Dog

—Anton Chekhov

Single ladies of a certain age—
Cass and Anne and Sandy and Liz,
widows, divorcees, spinsters all—
stroll around our neighborhood,
their pooches on leashes,
as if lifelines in hand,
babytalking to their dogs as they go.

Once Sandy told me she hopes
Rosalind outlives her, though it's unlikely,
given the lifespan of pets,
and the other day Anne came sobbing
up onto my front porch,
heartbroken that Hannah had just died—
sudden unexpected heart failure.
(In fact, I'd seen them on the street
only the other day, healthy animals both,
Hannah pulling Anne along
as if she were a sled driver, arm outstretched,
nearly yanked from its socket.)
I remembered my cats' demise
twenty years ago,
how accelerated and inevitable it seemed,
death sped up like the final reel of a film.

But when Cass's Benny died,
it only took her three weeks
to replace him with Elmo
from the animal rescue shelter,
and now she seems happy again,
tugged along the sidewalk
as if to her destiny,
a plastic poop bag around her wrist.

# Age

"I remember you from years ago,"
I greeted the pretty blond girl
behind the desk at the gym
when I swiped in my ID card,
here for my morning swim.

"You look great!" Karen gushed,
as if she meant it,
a woman less than half my age.

Later, on my way out,
I asked how long it had been
since she last worked at this club.

"Six years in November," she answered.
"I was at the Canton club a year
before I moved to California.
I've been back six months,
but I just started here again last week."

Karen's curves, hair, skin,
snappy blue eyes, sassy personality
had been the talk of the men's locker room,
a real looker, a knockout.
I recalled the time I'd cut my hand
and she'd helped me bandage it up.

"You look great!" she exclaimed again.
"I mean it. You don't look
like you've aged a bit!"

"Thank you!" I smiled, leaving the gym,
knowing I'd aged another six years.

# Full Disclosure

"The only brown hair on my body
is the hair on my head,"
the girl in line in front of me
at Chipotle told her two companions,
another girl and a boy,
all three college students,
her tone matter-of-fact,
nothing suggestive in her voice.
She might have been talking
about the literature exam
or the biology lab experiment.

"Thanks for sharing,"
the other girl's sarcastic response,
but I couldn't help thinking
of the hair elsewhere
on the brown-haired girl's body.
Blond? Black? Red?

I wasn't sure if I'd tag that
with an LOL or a TMI,
but I remembered my Facebook friend
Ramona posting last night:
"Anxious about the biopsy
performed on my left boob this morning."

She Knew Exactly How I Felt

# Heimlich

When the man at the next table
reared up like a wounded bear,
staggered around his overturned chair,
hands at his throat,
eyes terrified, face red,

and Paul, the waiter, rushed over,
swift as a dancer right on cue,
grabbed the man from behind,
as if supporting his partner's body
in some intricate ballroom routine,
spun him in place, a graceful chassé,
lifted and then squeezed,
the chunk of meat flying from his throat,
landing by my shoe,

all I could think of
was Billy Hunter
from high school
with the high girl voice.
For years we jeered, "Faggot,"
until we learned
when he was a child,
choking on a piece of food,
his father had tried removing it
with a coathanger.

# The Hairball

"You know how sometimes
you feel like if you can just
cough that last bit of gunk
out of your lungs,
you'll get over that cold,
or at least be able to breathe?

"Our marriage was like that.
If we could just get past
that last hairball,
things would be smooth,
we'd be able to breathe."

"So what did you do?
How did you clear your throat?
Sex?"

"Oh yeah,
but that's never enough, is it?
Sure, it brings you closer
for a while,
but it's no hairball."

# The Sensitive Poet

"Have I ever gotten emotional
when I was giving a poetry reading?
One time last summer
I had to hike to the bookstore
where I was a featured reader
in hundred-degree heat,
hot winds whipping dust everywhere.

"I drank a glass of water
when I got there,
figured I'd be OK,
but about a minute into the reading
my eyes started tearing up,
and then my nose started running,
and then it was like
I'd just started bawling.

"I was reading a poem
about trading in my old car
I'd had for a dozen years,
looking at it in the rearview
as I drove off the lot in another.
I think maybe the people there
thought there were more layers
to the poem than there really were.
You know, hidden meanings.

"I had to cut the reading short
because nobody had any tissues,
and I didn't want to blow my nose
into the sleeve of my shirt.
Later, one of the people in the audience
told me she knew exactly how I felt."

# Chode

*A chode is primarily described as a short and stubby penis, often wider than it is long. A fool, a jerk.*

—Urban Slang Dictionary

Standing in line at Starbuck's
I overheard the two girls talking.

"Vivian said he was a chode,"
the blond girl in running shorts shrugged.

"I didn't get a good impression of him either,"
commented her Asian companion in the Stanford t-shirt.

A *chode?*
Whatever it was, it didn't sound very flattering.
I paid for my latte and went out to my car.
The word bothered me all the way home.
I Googled it as soon as I got in.
A definition popped up in the urban dictionary.
So *that's* a "chode"?

I wondered at the etymology of the term.
Polari slang dating back to the 1950's,
the lingo of British circus performers,
sailors and prostitutes, gay subculture,
from a Hindi word for "fuck,"
brought to Britain via the Raj.
*Not* in the OED, of course—
except as the past tense of "chide."

*Who knew?*

# A Close Shave

*"People who shave grow a day younger every morning."*
—Vladimir Nabokov, *Mary*

"You're not supposed to shave in the steamroom."

All lathered up,
feeling my whiskers relax
like moviegoers slumping in their seats,
clutching my razor,
I open my eyes to the muscular young man
hovering over me where I sit on the bench
in the clouds of steam,
a towel swaddled about his waist,
reminding me of the street-crossing guards
in elementary school,
their bright orange vests
their air of faux authority.

"No problem," I lie,
casual as a kid playing hooky,
but feeling like the busted jaywalker,
hurtled back in time half a century.
"I'm just softening my whiskers.
I'll shave out at the washbasins."

"OK, sorry," the kid apologizes,
"It's just that it's against the rules.
Health Department."

As he turns away,
I check the impulse to trip him,
like a sixth-grade bad boy
on the edge of puberty,
anticipating the day
he'll be able to shave like a man.

# Working Class Hero

The year Lennon released his first solo album,
*Plastic Ono Band,* October, 1970,
I was working at a Capitol Records plant
in Jacksonville, Illinois,
slipping lp's into cardboard sleeves,
putting them on the conveyor belt
for Mary and Kristin,
two farmers' wives making extra money
now that the crops were in.

Mary and Kristin checked the albums for flaws,
stacked them into boxes,
put the boxes onto palettes
for the forklift guy to tote away.

Seething with moral outrage, Mary,
an enormous woman in a nest of cardboard boxes,
like a hippo wading in shallow river water,
jabbed a meaty finger at the back cover
where the lyrics were printed:
*but you're still fucking peasants as far as I can see.*

"Look at that!" she spat at Kristin,
I was afraid she'd tear the records apart
like those Southern Baptists
stamping on Beatles records
when Lennon said they were more popular than Jesus.
But she restrained herself, only snorting her wrath,
blowing her indignation like a large river mammal.

Kristin, a younger woman, Mary's protégé,
had a subversive streak:
maybe she drove to work and home with Mary,
out to their lonely country homes,

but she asserted independence, an open mind:
Kristin and I exchanged looks
over Mary's bent-double body,
rolling our eyes.

# Stu

That summer on the college paint crew
the older guys, the lifers,
Hiram, Clark and Luther,
called me "Stu."
They all swore I reminded them
of somebody they used to work with named Stu.

We climbed into the back of the pickup,
ladders, rollers, cans of latex—
beige, turquoise, mint green, and white—
packed into the bed with us,
headed for the dorms.
"You clean up the brushes, Stu?"

A slender college boy with long hair,
my sex life was open to speculation.
Hiram wanted to know if I had a girlfriend;
Clark wondered if I'd been getting any.
I demurred, feeling assaulted.
How was this their business?
It didn't help that I *wasn't* "getting any."

"You don't like takin' da honeys out?" Luther kidded.

"My body wouldn't like that," I joked back.

After a pregnant pause, Luther asked,
voice confidential as a conspirator,
 "Do *he* take you out?"

Puzzled, I asked, "Who?"

"Your buddy," Luther answered, the sweat
beading up in the wrinkles of his brown forehead.

"My *body*," I clarified, "I said my *body*."

Luther chuckled then, winked at Clark.
I suddenly had an idea
what it was about Stu
these workmen saw in me.

# Study Buddies

As we crammed together in the library
for the History exam,
my study buddy Kelly Anne said
she loved him because he suffered so,
but who knows
why one person falls for another?
(How I loved her scent—
Soap? Shampoo? Perfume? Exciting!
Side by side, our thighs
warmed each other at the big oak table.)

His name was Rocky,
not the name you think of
for a sensitive guy.

"When one of those fundraisers
comes on the TV,
the ones that show
abused animals in cages?
Rocky has to cover his eyes,
and I turn down the volume.
I let him know when it's over.
It's really heartbreaking."

Part of me admired the guy,
tenderheartedness an endearing trait,
but could she really love him for that?
For blubbering about lab animals?

Yes, she was his girlfriend.
Was this some kind of jealousy?
It was: After the History exam,
I started studying with Michelle instead.

# Registering to Vote

The Twenty-sixth Amendment
giving 18-year-olds the right to vote
wouldn't be ratified
for another six months,
but Congress had amended the Voting Rights Act
allowing 18-year-olds the right
in federal elections, just that summer,
so, back home in Michigan on Christmas break
from freshman year at college,
a buddy and I went
to Potawatomi Rapids City Hall
to register with the clerk,
like refugees from *Alice's Restaurant*.
I'd taken a tab of LSD
about an hour before.

Standing at the glass window
as if waiting in line for a ticket at the movie,
chatting with the middle-aged lady,
it all seemed so suddenly hilarious to me;
the woman appeared as Granny Clampett to me,
the *Beverly Hillbillies* matriarch
played by the vaudevillian Irene Ryan,
and I began howling with laughter,
tears in my eyes, doubled over,
Gary aghast by my side.
Oh, how invulnerable I felt!

"I don't know what's so funny,"
the woman sniffed,
clearly miffed by the scruffy college kid.
I bit my lips,
trying to hold in my elation
until after we'd signed our documents and left.

*I was free! I was free!*

I hadn't been looking for God,
but this was a moment of transcendence.

# Justice

My college friends and I all took heart
when the Supreme Court voted 5-4
in favor of the teenager who wore the jacket
with FUCK THE DRAFT on the back
when he walked through a courthouse corridor
on his way to a courtroom.
Protected by the First and Fourteenth Amendments.
It was 1971. Our student deferments
wouldn't last forever,
but sometimes it felt like the war would.

"One man's vulgarity is another's lyric,"
Justice John Marshall Harlan wrote
in the decision to overturn the ruling.
The kid, Paul Cohen, had been convicted
of disturbing the peace,
sentenced to thirty days in jail.

When the case was remanded for formal dismissal,
Cohen had to return to the court.
"The judge was upset
with the Supreme Court's ruling,"
he recalled years later,
"but I probably angered him more
when I asked for my jacket back."

# Sit-Down Comics

"Many heart attacks occur
while sitting on the toilet,"
the emergency response trainer told us,
and he mentioned the vagus nerve,
which slows the heart rate,
causing cardiac arrest.

I thought he said "Vegas,"
and thought, how appropriate:
always a crap shoot.

I forget how he linked this
to sitting on the toilet,
but I was already thinking
of famous toilet-sitting deaths anyway.
Elvis, found dead
on his bathroom floor, naked,
having crawled a few feet from the can.
Lupe Velez, too,
but hers was suicide, sleeping pills.
I remembered Warhol's movie about her.
Lenny Bruce likewise OD'd on the toilet,
heroin in his case.
Catherine the Great, Evelyn Waugh,
the eleventh century King of England,
Edmund II: all toilet deaths.

Ah, the ignominy:
always a slight snicker
accompanying the revelation,
life reduced to a ridiculous gag,
death the punchline.

# Bay State Road Blues

Upon listening to the Rolling Stones' *Blue and Lonesome* for the first time.

Remember that time, forty years ago,
when we bought Hohner blues harp harmonicas,
got high on weed, wailed
what we thought inspired music
in that student studio apartment I had
near Kenmore Square, across the street
from the dormitory where they said
Joan Baez had lived?
Or was it Martin Luther King?
Or both?

We fancied ourselves Chicago bluesmen,
Muddy Waters, Howlin' Wolf, Jimmy Reed, Little Walter,
full of soul,
our next move to busk
on the Common or the Public Garden,
or on the Esplanade by the Charles River,

until the girl in the apartment next to mine—
was her name Linda?—
pounded on the flimsy particleboard door,
threatened to call the landlord
*if you don't stop making that noise!*

# Existentialism

I was fifteen the summer of *Sergeant Pepper,*
swept away by the genius imagery,
the voices of the protagonists of the songs—
the lonely guy Ringo portrayed
in "With a Little Help from My Friends,"
the bored man in Lennon's "Good Morning Good Morning,"
the desperate girl in "She's Leaving Home."

That fall, my hip tenth grade English teacher,
Mrs. Fry, encouraged me to write my term paper
on the Beatles. The result?
*"Sergeant Pepper's Lonely Hearts Club Band:*
a Study in Existentialism."
I'd read an essay in *The Columbia Journalism Review,*
a periodical to which my father subscribed,
in which the writer used the term,
but I didn't have a clue
what "existentialism" was.

I called one of my father's colleagues at the college,
Dr. Hart, who patiently tried to explain
existence versus essence, Sartre, Kierkegaard,
the individual as a free agent determining
his own purpose in a world without meaning,
alienation, Nothingness or Death,
all very abstract to a teenager
who just admired the music.

Focusing on "A Day in the Life*,"*
I wrote about the alienation of the moviegoer
*(I saw a film today, oh boy…),*
like the character in the Walker Percy novel,
one step removed from reality—*alienated.*
Somehow I managed ten pages.

"Isn't the album really about mysticism and drugs?"
Mrs. Fry wrote at the bottom of my paper.
But she gave me an A.
I felt like I'd gotten away with something.

# A Pocketful of Mumbles

*"I am just a poor boy and my story's seldom told."*
—Paul Simon, "The Boxer"


I'd come to Boston from the provinces,
after graduating from college with a liberal arts degree,
looking for a job.  But I got no offers.

Renting a room at the Charlesgate,
a roominghouse in Kenmore Square,
cheap weekly and monthly rates,
I answered help wanted ads,
the classifieds in the *Boston Globe*
like Chinese fortune cookies generating dreams.

At the time, before it became a dormitory
for Emerson College, unknown to me,
oblivious to my big-city surroundings,
some Charlesgate tenants ran drug and prostitution rings.

One evening, coming home
with the cheesesteak sub that would be my dinner,
I got on the elevator in the lobby
with a man and woman huddled in one corner.
The scruffy man, in a greasy bop cap,
rope-veined arms, pushed the woman's arm
hard against her back, twisting, while she pled,
doubled over, "Please, Sonny, don't. I'm sorry.
You're hurting me! Please don't."

A kid from the sticks
with old-fashioned ideas about women,
I muttered to the man
he should leave her alone.

Glaring at me past the curtain
of her uncombed bleach-blond hair,
the girl's voice toughened like a cinched rope.
"Mind your own fuckin' business," she snarled.

The door opened to my floor.
I got off the elevator,
mumbling something
about having a good evening.

# Fifi

When I read about the accident,
Glen tumbling off his roof
like Icarus falling out of the sky,
slamming into the pavement
three stories down,
snapping his neck,
dying instantly,

I remembered the fey lad in Boston,
just out of the closet
where he'd shut himself up
for the first nineteen years
of his Midwestern life,
glorying in his new-found freedom
hundreds of miles from home,
carrying around a stuffed armadillo
he called Fifi,
a leash around its neck,
the hilarity he and his friends found
in the shocked, bewildered expressions
of the other commuters on the subway trains,
a sort of smug contempt
for the provincials' lack of imagination.

Icarus, yes: precocious, careless, proud,
sure he could repair his chimney
all by himself, without assistance,
pleased with himself
for the ingeniousness of Fifi.

# Liking It Hot

*"I'm gonna be twenty-five in June. That's a quarter of a century.
Makes a girl think."*

—Sugar in *Some Like It Hot*

Maybe because I'm in my mid-twenties,
an age when most people
in my grandparents' generation
already had a houseful of kids,
my grandpa's anxious I get hitched;
maybe he wants to cuddle
a great-grandchild before he dies.

I'm in an on-again, off-again
with this guy I work with,
lately mostly on,
but we don't have any plans.

I don't know what Grandpa knows about Martin;
maybe my mom mentioned him
when they talked on the phone.
But a few months back Grandpa wrote me a letter—
they live in the Bible belt,
a small town outside Louisville—
telling me God told him and Grandma
I was going to marry this year.
He said they wanted to meet my man
to make sure he was "saved."

During our pillow talk one night,
I told this to Martin.
For a second, I could have sworn
his eyes darted around like a cat's
looking for a way to escape.
Then he laughed.

# Boo Coo

Once the star halfback in high school,
Duncan came back from Vietnam
a changed man:  slept in a hammock
he'd strung up in the woods by the river,
cut his own hair with a knife,
the locks uneven clumps and patches,
smoked weed all day long.

With Duncan, everything was "boo coo"—
Vietnamese slang for "beaucoup"
he'd picked up in-country.
He told everybody he smoked boo coo dope,
liked to get boo coo high,
had gotten boo coo Asian pussy in Nam.
Boo coo this, boo coo that.

His girlfriend, Linda Swanson, head cheerleader
when they were in school, who'd vowed
to wait for him until he got out of service,
dumped him after one date when he returned,
soon engaged to dull George Shedd,
assistant manager at the A&P grocery.

"Sad what happened to Dunc," she sighed,
wiping an invisible tear from her cheek,
but that's all she'd say.

One morning we woke to the news.
Duncan, dressed in camo, set fire
to Shedd's rancher out on 27-Mile Road
while he and Linda were inside having supper,
beat George half to death with a baseball bat,
begged Linda on his knees to take him back,
shot himself in the side of the head

when all she could do was cry,
shake her head back and forth—
*no, no, no*—
her long blond hair whipping like snakes.

# Joyeux Noël

Her eyes alight with mischief,
as if laughing at some private joke,
Miss Brooks stood at our door
that cold December morning
offering a French grammar textbook
to my mother, who'd answered the doorbell.

"Please give this to David," she smiled,
turning back to her car.
"I won't need it until
the new semester begins at the high school."

My brother, home from college
for the Christmas holidays,
had gone out with his buddies
the night before, stumbling in drunk
well past midnight, my father cautioning
my angry mother that David
just needed to blow off some steam
after his grueling freshman semester.

When he saw Miss Brooks' car
at the curb, David had darted up the stairs
like a frightened cat, slamming himself
into his room, cowered behind the closed door.

Miss Brooks was the hottie French teacher
rumored to buy beer
for the boys on the football team,
whispered to do so much more for them.

"I didn't know you were taking French,"
my mother's voice colder
than the Michigan winter outside,
handing him the copy of *Aujourd'hui.*

"I'm thinking about auditing a class
in the spring," David mumbled,
never letting on he and his friends
had banged on their teacher's door
late the night before, thinking
they were in for a different kind of lesson.

# My First Sex Scandal

I spat out my coffee, laughing
when I read, in her obituary,
Mandy Rice-Davies' description of her life:
"one slow descent into respectability."

I was ten when the Profumo affair
hit the newspapers; the Kennedy brothers'
infidelities stayed secret for years to come.
It baffled me how a whole government
could crumble from such an indiscretion,
even if a Soviet spy was mixed up in it.
Prime Minister MacMillan would resign
later that year, the Tories in tatters.
It wasn't even he who'd had sex
with the teenaged Christine Keeler.

At the trial spawned from the scandal,
aristocratic Lord Astor denied
he'd had sex with Christine's friend Mandy.
From the witness box she'd shot back:
"Well, he would, wouldn't he?"

Even at ten I admired her spunk,
a girl who'd left school at fifteen
to work as a department store model.
She'd wind up as wealthy
as the upper crust men
whose reputations she'd ruined.

# Swann's Way

Coming up the airplane aisle,
looking for her assigned seat,
an overhead storage bin,
like a kid at camp, or a refugee,
the pretty Asian college girl
clutched not just a book—
all the others held laptops,
e-readers, ear buds, "mobile devices"—
but a copy of *Swann's Way*.

I couldn't resist saying to her,
from the seat I'd already taken,
"Marcel Proust! Hey, I'm impressed!"

The girl blushed, looking at her book,
then over her shoulder at her boyfriend,
a pudgy white guy, likewise looking
for his seat assignment, overhead storage,
"He's reading it, too."
The boy rolled his eyes.
*What's she doing with* him, *anyway?*

During the two-hour flight,
I glanced at her in a seat across the aisle,
her head bowed over the paperback,
and I remembered Aika Morita,
a girl from my college days
I never quite worked up the nerve
to ask out on a date.

After we'd landed, recovered our bags,
idled in the aisle, waiting to exit,
I heard the girl, behind me, exasperated,
"All he does is take a walk at Combray,
admiring the hawthorns!"

"No way I'm reading that book,"
the boyfriend declared.
*What a douche!*

I felt so keenly then how
I could never recover that lost time.

# Invisible to the Young

One of the last passengers
on the flight to Detroit,
I managed to snare an aisle seat
a few rows from the back of the plane.

"This flight is completely full,"
the stewardess announced again.
She'd warned us at least eight times;
it could have been a recorded message.
"Please take the first available seat.
so that we can leave on time."

Like shoppers in a produce market
the last stragglers trolled the aisle
for the best possible seat
as if looking for the finest melon.
*Please take the seat next to me*
I prayed to the college girl
in a University of Michigan T-shirt.

I remembered the girl I'd sat next to
on a Greyhound bus to New York
one New Year's Eve forty years ago.
We kissed when I left the bus at Hempstead,
our tongues touching.

But the girl on the airplane
looked right past me—
a middle-aged bald guy with a book—
and took a seat between two women.
The fat guy coming up behind her
squeezed into the seat next to me.

# Winter Tune-up

Coming up from the basement,
I recognize the *doo-doo-do-do-doooo* opening bar
of "Strangers in the Night," whistled
in an absent-minded birdcall.
by the guy from the fuel company,
here to tune up the furnace for the winter.

*Doo-doo-do-do-doooo.*
As far as he goes.  Over and over.
A blast from the furnace
when he jacks up the thermostat.
*Doo-doo-do-do-doooo,*
up and under like a pre-dawn cricket song.

*Exchanging glances* floats through my brain
in a Sinatra voice. *Something something*
*What were the chances?*

A pop song from half a century ago.
Always heard it was about a gay tryst,
but it seemed to me
it could just as easily be a man and a woman.

Gary, the furnace guy,
looks to be in is early thirties,
young enough to be my son.
Odd, I think, he's whistling that song.

*Two lonely people, we were*
*doo-doo-do-do-dooo.*

After an hour, Gary trudges up the steps,
lugging his toolbox and equipment.
"Okay, replaced the oil filter,
installed a new nozzle,
did basic maintenance on the boiler system.
You're good to go. Sign here and here."

Our fingers touch when he hands me the pen.
A spark of static electricity.
"Whoa!" Gary apologizes.
"Must be from working on the boiler."
We exchange a glance.

# What I Enjoyed

From the blue ink anchor tattoo
on the man's meaty tanned forearm,
I took the burly railroad maintenance guy
to be a veteran of the Navy or Marines.
I was standing on the platform in Hoboken
waiting for my PATH train
to the World Trade Center station.

Like a Song Sparrow, he absently whistled
a sweet trilling tune over and over again:
*dee-dee-dee-da-dee-dee deeeee-deeee..*
*dee-dee-dee-da-dee-dee deeeee-deeee..*

It sounded so familiar, but just out of reach.
As if I were a blind man
figuring out the identity of a thing by touch,
I groped the sounds he whistled
but couldn't quite identify the song.

When my train came, I took a seat,
opened my newspaper for the ten-minute ride,
but I couldn't get the ditty out of my head.
And then the words came to me,
like a photograph materializing in the developer tray:
*I'm strictly a female female…*
*I'm strictly a female female…*
The song? "I Enjoy Being a Girl"
from the Broadway musical, *Flower Drum Song,*
a tune my mother sang in snatches
driving me to school half a century ago.

Stepping into the bustle of the financial district,
I can still see her
behind the wheel of the beige Dodge Dart
back home in Potawatomi Rapids, Michigan.
*I'm strictly a female female...*
*dee-dee-dee-da-dee-dee deeeee-deeee..*

# Ribald

The blurb on the back of the 1971 novel,
from a contemporary review, declared,
"A ribald celebration of girlhood."
I realized I hadn't seen that word
in print, for decades.  Was it just me?
A term I associated with *Playboy Magazine*
jokes about women with enormous breasts,
cheating husbands, risqué *nudge wink* quips.

First used in the thirteenth century,
*ribaud,* a Middle English scoundrel, a lecher,
from Old French *riber,* debauched,
akin to Old High German *riban,*
to copulate—literally, to rub.

Bawdy, lascivious, lewd, smutty,
racy, salacious, salty, kinky,
suggestive, barnyard, scurrilous, hard core:
more familiar words take its place.

Has the word died, now?
Here lies Ribald, 1300-2000, R.I.P.

(Or do words ever die,
as long as there are voices to speak them,
eyes to read them?)

Still, the word was a siren;
the blurb lured me in:
I bought a copy of the book.

# Animal Reactions

"Reggie!"

Only after his name
ripped from my throat
in unexpected recognition,
as unpremeditated as a bird call,
in the thronging anonymity
of the shopping mall,

did I realize Reggie
had seen me first,
scurrying past like a rodent,
eyes averted,
trying to avoid me:
the sham look of surprise
so painfully fake.

We chatted a few minutes
about our children—
fathers of high school classmates—
before parting company.

Animal instinct told me
Reggie just didn't like me.
Up until then
I hadn't thought of him
one way or the other.

Now I hated him.

# Rigoletto

*We was at Rigoletto's,*
I thought, passing the musclebound guy
talking into a cellphone
in the locker room, on my way to the showers:
my mental shorthand for a goon,
a line spoken by Spats Columbo's bodyguard
in *Some Like It Hot.*
His head was like a pebble
on top of boulder-like shoulders,
chest rippling with a strength
the term "six-pack" didn't do justice.

"Thesis, antithesis, synthesis,"
he was saying into the phone,
"Hegelian dialectic. You're thinking
more in terms of the Socratic method,
argumentative dialogue, question and answer,
to stimulate critical thinking,
though both describe a process
for arriving at truth,
but really, isn't Hegel's logic
more provisional, truth evolving?"

I looked at the guy again.
*We was at Rigoletto's:*
Spats' alibi he was at the opera
confirmed by his henchman.
I went past the showers to the sauna,
where I sat on the hot wooden bench,
chin on fist, like Rodin's *The Thinker.*

Glad All Over

# What Is a Solofie?

Driving my children to school,
I popped in a Dave Clark Five CD,
the bubblegum music of my era.

"Glad All Over," "Catch Us if You Can,"
"Because," "Everybody Knows," "Bits and Pieces":
Middle schoolers, Anna and Zoe swooned.

We listened to the CD all week.
One morning, when the DC5
launched into "You Got What It Takes,"

one of the girls asked,
"Daddy, what's a 'solofie'?"
*What's a what?*

"He says, 'you got what it takes
to satisfy. You got what it takes
to set my solofie.'"

I thought about the word,
a *solofie.* The girl in the song
"set" his solofie.

She satisfied him;
she set his solofie.
She had what it took to do it.

The pornographic possibilities
set my brain on fire,
but of course I had to resist.

"Soul on fire," I explained.
"The girl sets his *soul,*"
I clarified, *"on fire."*

# Father's Day on Facebook

Anita kicks off the thread.
*Is anybody here as conflicted*
*about Father's Day as I am?*
Then Carol calls her dad a paedophile,
spelling it the way that screams: "Psychiatric disorder!"
"Nuff said," she concludes, laconic.
Mary laments her father'd abandoned
her and her brother when she was five.
"But good riddance. He was violent and cruel."

I remember the tabloid headline:
Girl in Coma for Three Years
Wakes Up and Reveals Horrifying Secret.
Yeah, the father did it—
the girl's mom's boyfriend.
You don't want to know the details.

My father disdained Mother's and Father's Day—
"Inventions of the department stores," he sneered,
"to make more money
selling junk people don't need."

Can you blame him?
An historian, he was pushing sixty
when Nixon made Father's Day official.
How he loathed Tricky Dick already!

I decide not to add my two cents,
probably not worth even that,
but I know, with the bar set so low,
I probably wasn't such a bad dad myself.

# The Full Lotus

Maybe no one will notice,
I thought, looking down my legs.
After all, I *was* wearing an extra-large T-shirt;
it fell over my hips like a skirt.
Plus, my black Hanes briefs
*did* sort of resemble gym shorts. *Sort of.*
I remembered the dreams
from puberty, naked in a classroom,
and nobody's noticed yet.

In preparing for the Wednesday
evening yoga class my wife and I attend,
I had forgotten to put on shorts
before I pulled on my jeans.
I only discovered this now,
after we'd driven to the studio.
The class was about to start.

I won't even attempt a head stand,
I thought, going through possible poses
in my head, placing my mat
in the back of the room.
I closed my eyes,
the classic ostrich strategy—
if I couldn't see the others,
they couldn't see me.
I felt a tap on my shoulder,
opened my eyes.

"Put these on," my wife advised,
handing me my jeans.

"I removed your keys and wallet,
took off the belt. You'll be fine."

I'm sure she saw the gratitude
competing with my embarrassment.
At least she wasn't laughing.

# You Made a Fool of Everyone

On the last day of meditation class,
Josh, the beatific instructor,
began with a Zen parable
about mindfulness.

After ten years of practice,
a novice approached the Zen master
to gauge his progress.
"It's raining out," the Zen master observed.
"When you came in,
did you leave your umbrella
beside your right sandal or your left?"
The student bowed to the master.
"I will return in another ten years."

After a moment, Abby raised her hand.
Josh nodded to her.

"Does this mean
once we've achieved mindfulness
we'll never lose another umbrella?"

Josh's expression was enigmatic,
the silence awkward.
Was she being sarcastic or just dense?
Was she mocking him, or was she serious?

I remembered the old Beatles song:
*If looks could kill*
*it would have been us*
*instead of him...*

# The Metamorphosis

In my eyes she changed
from dumpy to masculine
the moment she mentioned
Natalia, her roommate.

When I first met Kimberly,
four weeks ago,
my new boss at work,
a woman in her mid-thirties,
the stiff pantsuits seemed
just a management uniform,
the short red hair
pulled painfully back off her face,
crisp as the creases in her pants,
merely a mask of authority.

But all at once
Kim seemed to be dressing in drag,
like a character from *Cabaret*.
Not that I'm judgmental—
if anything, I admire her more
for the burdens her orientation brings—
but  how sudden the transformation
when we talked
over the conference table in her office,
and she mentioned Natalia,
her "roommate."

When she mentioned her boyfriend,
she turned back into an office manager.

# How Joe McElroy Met His Wife

When the fire alarm went off
at three in the morning,
we all fled like roaches from a bug bomb
out of our rooms at the Charlesgate,
down the stairwells in bathrobes and slippers,
even the crippled girl in 303,
frail legs tapering like spindles,
propping herself on crutches,
grasshopper-like in her lunges
down the carpeted hallway.

From the threshold at the entrance on Kenmore Square,
I saw the firetrucks' red-blue whirligig
through a light scrim of March snow
stirring up the residents' panic
like kernels in a popcorn popper,
before we were herded out into the cold,
where we swarmed about the wet sidewalk,
the damp seeping into my slippers.

Then I saw Janine, hovering like a honeybee
in the hive of a building crevice, barefoot,
dancing from one foot to the other,
and I forgot all about my own discomfort,
drawn to her like a drone to the queen.

I offered her a slipper to stand in,
and we both stood stalk-like on one leg,
propped against each other,
a pair of praying mantises,
until we were allowed back in: false alarm.

Janine lived two floors above me,
a room I came to know well
in the months to come
before we rented
a Beacon Hill one-bedroom together.

# Rashida and the Beast

When the coronavirus spread like oil
from a wounded tanker in the Mediterranean,
through the country and around the world,
I had to move my animals
from the circus in Suez
where we'd been performing
to our desert compound outside Cairo,
eight lions and three tigers,
around six thousand feline pounds,
not easy for a 130-pound woman and her entourage!

But I love my job,
dressed in my leopard-skin body suit,
high black leather boots,
wielding the batons and whips of my profession
like some badass dominatrix on Broadway;
but there's nothing to it, really,
coaxing my babies through rings of fire,
charming them to walk over my body
as I lie spread-eagled in the ring.
Like any man, give them affection
and morsels of donkey meat,
and they'll do anything for you!

Lions and tigers are so much easier
to deal with than the schoolchildren
and their swaddled-up mothers
who come to our shows.
As another famous lion tamer,

Maria Rasputin, once observed
when asked why she did it,
"Why not? I have been in a cage with Bolsheviks."

So now we wait out the Plague,
a more deadly killer than men or wild animals.

# Gongoozling

A new word for me—
standing apparently idle in the towpath
watching the slow, slow progress
of the boats in the UK canal
here near Evesham, by the Avon River.

"Possibly from the Lancashire dialect,"
my friend Tony tells me,
"the words *gawn* and *goozle*
meaning to gawp or stare."

I remember my mother's
gradual descent into old age,
the same canal down which we all travel;
the day my brother and I "reasoned"
with her to give up her car.
She was past ninety then.

"Face it, Ma, you rarely drive as it is.
Kate and Becky take you to the grocery
whenever you need to shop."
Her grown granddaughters, in town.
"Think of the money you'll save
on insurance and maintenance."

But all she saw: losing her independence,
just as all I see,
here in the towpath,
the slow, slow progress
through the locks.

# Wheel of Fortune

I didn't enter Sister Faye's
Psychic Readings shop
like Harry Houdini,
exposing frauds and charlatans,
but I didn't expect to contact
spirits of the dead, either.

Curiosity and a dare made me do it:
my friend Holly challenged me
when I sent her a cellphone photo,
the storefront with the neon outline
of a cross-legged, turbaned swami,
the words "Tarot Readings" and "Fortunes"
blinking on and off,
the "t" in "Fortunes" dead
as a cigarette ash.

Incense smothered like a chloroform-soaked hankie,
but I took a seat on the low stool,
gazing hopefully across the candles
guttering on the glass-topped table.

"Your mother misses you," Sister Faye soothed.
Not a far-fetched guess about my mom,
me a guy in his mid-sixties.
Besides, nobody said she was dead.

But I remembered the last time
I saw my mother, in hospice,
after the multiple organ failure,
several years ago now.

She lay doped-up in a hospital bed,
mostly unconscious, incoherent when awake,
no final moment of recognition.

"Tell her I miss her, too."

# Cyber Immortality

What a surprise to turn on
my computer this morning
to find an e-mail from my mother,
nothing in the Subject line
but her name in boldface,
indicating an unread message,
with a time and date stamp
from the night before.

Dead for more than half a year,
her house sold, estate settled.

I remembered reading similar stories,
people receiving e-mails from dead lovers,
their anguish, accompanied by photos of faces
shattered by grief, scarred with tears.
Taken by surprise,
for a nano-second—
a computer-era measurement—
I felt unalloyed joy,
before memory took over.

Still, this was not a malicious hoax.
Whoever hacked her Yahoo account
never knew my mom,
let alone if she was living or dead.
The e-mail left a residue,
the memory of happier times,
exchanging e-mails, sharing news.

Maybe this is reincarnation
in the electronic age.
Maybe this is the Afterlife.

# Grace

Standing in Roy Rogers
Bright fluorescent stainless steel
Buying a couple of kids meals
Cheeseburger, fries, coke and a toy

An incoherent old man
Beneath a Braves baseball cap
Making coochy-coo noises
At my bewildered children
I can't understand a word he says
I smile and nod
As if one of us is an idiot

He has no teeth
His stubbled upper lip
Collapses in on emptiness
In a way he's downright frightening

But my children sense in him
A whining, abandoned dog
Sniffing around garbage cans
A mutt that merits kindness
An animal yearning for kindness

You see it in their eyes
Timid, bemused,
But not turning away

And you can see it in his mucous food smile
The eyes pleading for compassion
As though for some cheap trinket
Glittering in a child's packaged meal
Grace as tangible as a packet of ketchup

How I wish we could manufacture it,
Market it, sell it
How I wish we could just give it away

# Now You're the Metaphor

As a kid in Potawatomi Rapids,
I thrilled to the Memorial Day parade,
always held on May 30 in those days,
even when it wasn't on a Monday,
that first taste of summer in Michigan,
a late winter snowstorm less and less likely,
the imminent end of the school year.

White-whiskered Mister Engstrom,
veteran of the Spanish-American War,
rumored to have been a Rough Rider himself,
borne down Erie Street in a gas-guzzling convertible,
behind the high school marching band,
waving, looking a little vague, bewildered.
He was time itself; he was age personified.

Today my Medicare insurance kicks in.
In a week I will be sixty-five.

# About the Author

Charles Rammelkamp is Prose Editor for BrickHouse Books in Baltimore, where he lives with his wife, Abby. Rammelkamp is the author of several collections of "historical" or "biographical" poetry sequences, written in dramatic monologue form, including *Fusen Bakudan* (Time Being Books), about World War Two Japanese balloon bombs and leper colony missionaries in Vietnam; *Mata Hari: Eye of the Day* (Apprentice House), about the life and career of the World War I *femme fatale* spy; *American Zeitgeist* (Apprentice House), which deals with the populist politician and Scopes Trial buffoon, William Jennings Bryan; *Catastroika* (Apprentice House), another collection of dramatic monologues in the voices of Maria Rasputin, the mad monk's daughter, who escaped Russia after the Revolution and became a lion tamer for Ringling Brothers, and a fictional Jewish character, Sasha Federmesser, who likewise escapes and immigrates to Baltimore. A chapbook of poems about female sailors in the British Royal Navy from the 17th to the 19th centuries, *Jack Tar's Lady Parts* (Main Street Rag Press), is also written in this style.

Rammelkamp's poetry also includes lyrical and narrative collections, including *The Book of Life* (March Street Press) and an earlier collection from Kelsay, *Ugler Lee,* as well as several chapbooks—*Me and Sal Paradise* (FutureCycle Press), *Mortal Coil* (Clare Songbirds Publishing) and most recently, *Sparring Partners* (Moonstone Press).

He has also published a novel, *The Secretkeepers* (Red Hen Press), and a collection of short stories, *Castleman in the Academy* (March Street Press).

Now retired, his career included editorial work and technical writing in a variety of industries and government agencies. He was also on the adjunct English faculty at Essex Community College for ten years.

Charles and Abby are the parents of two daughters, Anna and Zoe, and grandparents of a girl, Paloma, and a boy, Emilio.

www.ingramcontent.com/pod-product-compliance
Lightning Source LLC
Chambersburg PA
CBHW070448090426
42735CB00012B/2487